Poetry
The lunatic anomaly
Gérald Odar

poetry

The lunatic anomaly

Gérald Odar

~ 5 ~

I prefer present thoughts
The future haunts me
And in the past...
I forget myself

Copyright © Gérald Odar - 2024
Tous droits réserver/All rights reserved
Gérald Odar
22100 Aucaleuc France
gerald.odar.auteur@gmail.com
ISBN : 978-2-9589580-8-4
Dépôt légal : septembre/september 2024

Welcome to "The lunatic anomaly": a collection of short stories, poems and prose. I offer you a mixture of emotions, laughter and tears. Here, everything mixes, life, death. The little fleeting moments of our daily lives combine with fantaisies, parallel possibilities that will never exist.

Part I : A little thought bubble

THE END

I will write the beginning later

Tears don't fade
the pain...

They dilute it,
at most

Memory,
real treasure chest
and
nightmare drawer

My thoughts are
speeding...
I have flashes
in the head

I must be
a puzzle piece
row in
the wrong box

I'm dragging my feet
I wear out my soles

I start to cry
when my emotions get tangled

Little paper mache man
which unravels

I'm just a kid
who has a dripping heart
through the eyes...
So stop calling me
Sir !

Is there not a counter for
forgotten memories?
There, where, I could
reclaim the sweet moments
that my failing memory
let it fade and...
disappear.

By mixing
tears and soap,
could i get small bubbles
of emotions that I could
blow and disperse
in the world?

I have too many dreams, they overflow
of my nights...

To spread
in my days

A late snail,
so in a hurry started to spin
I wonder if since
 he arrived

It's not me
who cries...

...This is my heart

Little calm moment seeks
letters written on paper...

To enjoy a little tea!

I like to hold my dreams
all against me
Without necessarily accomplishing them...
Caress them,
it's already feeling like I exist!

Can we be
rainbow
manufacturer
and colorblind?

I imagine silences that
not lacking in eloquence
I write them in braille on the canvas
of my sensitivity

Eyes streaming...
Flashed in full excess of
sadness
She stops on the side of the road
of his life...
The heart in distress

When the moon looks at me...
It intimidates me
When she's not there...
I feel a void!

I just have dreams
in the clouds
The head? You say
Oh? That ! I don't know
where she is

At night, cats are gray because
that they washed their pajamas
with those of mice

Sometimes, i think of this little
orphan grain of sand that I have
crossed at the beach
He felt so alone, so sad
His dream was to leave, far away,
to the mountain
Ah, how heavy my heart is
when I think of this little grain
of sand, so alone

My tears coagulate on my
tight lips
My eyes melt to see
this world burning
I will sleep in the ashes
This evening
Between your dreams
and my nightmares

And they never stopped
to kill peace

As if, calm
drove them crazy

Insomnia is a small
piece of night
who does not find
sleep!

Later, I will be...
A big old twisted tree,
planted majestically at
middle of a sunflower field
that the wind rocks
nonchalantly...
No more, no less

I hear a star crying...
I wish I had a ladder
quite large
to reach and console her

I'm not crying, no,
I make rain grow
from shards of my heart.
I stay with my feet in this
puddle that I create,
while knowing full well
that I don't know how to swim

Narrative emotions
lying on leaves,
will avoid my ship
the pitfalls

I would like
moon-glasses...
To discern dreams in the
mist !

To all these shy looks
who did not dare to speak
To all those lost kisses
and these caresses flown away

My pillow is broken

I wake up at night!

Nope...
I promise, I won't cry

I prepare my eyes to look
the world

I'm just a little drop
crystal clear in the ocean of
humanity...

...A drop that clings
desperately to others...
Because she doesn't know how to swim

And... for example...
If I retrace my steps...
And that I serve this child in
my arms...
And I tell him... that it's okay
go...
Is it that...
will my fears go away?

Like the Phoenix reborn
from his ashes

I will be reborn from my tears

Can we iron
little hearts
crumpled?

Part II : A drop of slightly salty water

My eyelids are clouds
My tears from the rain
Your smile, a sun
Tell me life is beautiful
Nope...
Tell me you love me

I slipped on my tears
My heart fell
It has become too heavy
Alone, I cannot raise it

When you leave me
Take me into your thoughts
I don't want to be alone
waiting for you.

I told him:
"My tender little heart exchanges
feelings versus good care. »

She smiled

Today,
 I have nothing to tell you...
So I offer you a sweet look
packed in a smile

I walk with melancholy
~
Just to change her mind

Heart in pieces
Sitting alone on a bench
He feeds the birds with his
feelings

The resonance of my footsteps
tunes into the feverish beats
from my heart...
When I walk away from you

You even miss time
He hangs around in your absence...
Until almost becoming
motionless
And me...
I become a statue

Life without you would be a
immense desert...
Where, I would drink from my
tears, with such a bitter taste

The little notches that are our
differences…

Are also the catchphrases of
our lives

With you, it's arrhythmia…
With every kiss, my pulse
accelerates…
You turn me upside down

My thoughts whisper to me your
first name
Sweet symphony which
accompany my unreason

When I'm alone,
I'm thinking of you
When you are there,
I think of us

Sometimes coincidences are
disturbing
For example, I met you
the same day as love

It's with thoughts
disheveled that I am
presented front of you
With a precise gesture, embellished with
your beautiful smile, you painted
my feelings

There are things that
cannot be explained...
Like the parallel universe
covered in softness
who hides in your arms

My heart ?
This receptacle where I pile up love,
joy, tears and fear of losing you?
He drums inside me...
thinking of you

If this is all just a dream
Above all, don't let go of my hand
I want us to wake up
together

...and in the crowd,
suddenly,
we feel alone...
terribly

I am the Big
You are the Bang
There were two of us
at the beginning
We will remain so
until the end of time

My feelings play
hopscotch
My heart on the skipping rope
and my passion for perched cats
It's been like that since you
My life has become a lesson in
recreation

The wind caresses me
The rain tickles me
The clouds whisper to me
The stars surround me
And the moon tells me my dreams

We traveled to countries
which do not exist
Never in our memories has this
will fade away

I walked through the maze of my
youth without knowing what I
was looking for
I missed your presence
While I didn't know
your existence,
I was already in your footsteps

Love is a joker
which sprinkles hearts
behind the back of reason

Part III : My thoughts spark

He enters as discreetly as possible.
His mother surprises him.
She asks him why he has a stupid smile on his
face.
 He shrugs his shoulders and takes refuge in his
room.
Lying on his bed, he repeats his first name over
and over.
 The taste of his lips on his lingers.
 He remembers the softness of her breasts.
He said to himself: Can't wait for tomorrow.

She sits on a bench in her parents' garden. The wind blows gently, making her long hair flutter lightly. His eyes stare at the swing from his childhood. Old boards held together by worn ropes sweep through the air. She smiles at the memories of good times. Then small tears flow down her cheeks. She places a hand on her stomach and says:

– You too, you will see, you will fly away on this swing.

I'm touched, it's over... I'm not going to escape unscathed this time. I hobble to my car, pressing hard on the wound. It's a real hemorrhage in there, it's dripping down my clothes and leaving a trail on the asphalt. I feel them flowing through my feverish fingers. All these feelings flowing and spreading... Damn, she touched my heart... I love her.

I like empty streets.

We hear the buildings bear witness
of the passage of lovers of yesteryear.

I might not save
not the world but
I'm writing others to escape to!

You, my first reader of all
The one who excites my creativity and fuels my
doubts I love our meetings and our hugs
You are the canvas and I the painter
I admit, often to you, I think
Very expensive and versatile blank page

– What is love? she asked him.
– Love is being with you and not giving a damn
about this world that is crumbling around us.

She wanders from lamppost to lamppost,
oscillating between light and shadow.
She smiles at passers-by without a face, without a
glance.
His thoughts collide with the walls of the
labyrinth that is his brain.
She just wants to have a bite to eat.
Little beggar from the city center.

Are there shops in nudist camps that only sell empty hangers?

A feeling of well-being envelopes him when he sees her passing in the street. Hidden behind her window, he blushes when she looks up. He gives her a little wave, she responds with a smile, like every morning.

I would like an after-sales service that erases the
torments,
 bad memories.
I wish the stone in the shoe of our self-esteem
could be easily removed.
I would love so much...

As far as I look, I only see
the echo of your name.

She is sitting on the old steps worn by time. Her back hurts, her heart makes her die. She watches people passing by, it's her hobby. She listens to people laughing, complaining, loving each other and arguing. All that, for her, is in the past. She lived, she doesn't have too many regrets, her children had children who have already grown up well. Sitting on the old steps worn by time, like her in the end, she awaits death, peacefully, it's her pastime.

With a few little ones
not much, you show me great moments.

As all the cabins were taken, I chose my life
without trying it. Sometimes she squeezes me, she
scratches me or she bothers me. But I manage to
put great people in it and they act like softener.
And then, my life, I am happy in it!

They remained children
and lived happily!

Amazed by the lapis lazuli glow in her eyes, he stammered out a compliment. The words stumbled from his clumsy lips. They rushed to be reduced to a thousand pieces on the flagstones of the public garden. He quickly got down on his knees to pick them up. But in vain, the dislocated letters were lost in the blowing breeze. He becomes silent for a moment and she, amused at this misfortune, smiles at him, moving on.

The vehicle moves quietly. Behind the laminated glass of the passenger compartment, a road passes through the woods. It's summer, finally, on the calendar, the sky is in a rather sulky mood. A small, not really important event slows down the car's progress: a squirrel crosses. It doesn't take much to feel a dose of well-being, placing a smile on your lips like a kiss. The frightened animal hastens to return to the thickets.

The apartment is quiet... since his recent departure, things are no longer the same. A look in the bathroom: clothes carelessly left on the floor near the laundry bin. It's "She", her way of doing things, her art of living. He misses her so much. He crossed the few meters that separate him from the kitchen area. He inserts a capsule... but hesitates before starting the coffee maker. The smell will cover the last scents of its perfume. He finally presses, resigned to waiting for her to return this evening after work.

The lost moments, the things we put off until tomorrow.
All this... Where is it going?
Is there a recycling system for this stuff?
I wonder...

Sea side,
lonely bench
looking for lovers to share precious moments

I could write about the stars, to be poetic.
Or, possibly on the moon, with romantic effect.
But I will instead reveal that I like to drink your
words into an idyllic coma.

Suddenly, one day, there is a person.
And the world may well stop turning
We'll keep dancing.

He knows full well that it exists, there, somewhere, in this vast world.

But he struggles to get through his door.

He is afraid of revealing himself to the eyes of the inhabitants of this planet.

So, he burrows into his cocoon, dreaming of becoming a butterfly.

She advances, or rather, she drags herself.

His head buried in his hood, no one sees his tears.

Today he told her it was over.

She had never supposed that there could be an expiration date on love.

His heart cries in color
Red pain

She closes the door, turns the key and thus locks her intimate world. She goes downstairs, checks to see if she has any mail: nothing... as usual.

Her heart sinks, she is already starting to get impatient for a letter the next day. She hides behind a smile when she meets her neighbors. She just hopes that he is well, her unwilling soldier gone far away.

The frantic race that he had started since his youth gave him points aside. He no longer knew why he was running out of steam, his only certainty was that his life depended on it... and there, in the dust, the traces left by the dreams he was pursuing.

No need to peel flowers to know that I love you madly.
My psychiatrist told me that!

Life has taken its toll on me,
so now I will write her until she likes me.

The rain lapped then trickled down the fogged window of the bus. The sky darkens as the day fades. She begins to recognize the setting: her old school, the village square, the small bakery. She gives a hint of a smile, imbued with little joy. The funeral and for tomorrow...

Tonight she won't sleep much. Not in this house that saw him grow up. The walls have too many things to remind him of.

The bus finally stops. She gets up and leaves, thanking the driver. The wind and the drops whip against her face, hiding her tears. His father welcomes him... alone.

This morning, I did my little market. I took a few of your smiles to brighten my day. I will hold them to my heart. I will return them to you with kisses in the evening.

The stars told me about you...
They miss you since you lived near me.

Breathing short, he spans the tens of meters of this long corridor. He left his job immediately as soon as he was informed of the call. His heart strikes like a blacksmith on an anvil. He missed his arrival, that's for sure... he blames himself. He hears her scream, he knows it's her. A smile covers his face, his head spins. He opens the door that was indicated to him. Behind: his wife... and his daughter, recently arrived among us. A rush of joy escapes from her eyes... She is there... There are three of them.

The store

I went into one of these souvenir shops. I asked
the craftsman who runs this shop to restore one
of mine. An old one, very soft, honeyed... One
where my mother held me against her, to comfort
me from a nightmare. One who reassures me and
gives me the courage to pursue my dreams... even
without her.

People in the real world find me friendly.
 They are nice and want to help me.
But for me, what I want...
It's calm for dreaming.
And that's it!

I can't let go, too many imaginary characters are
counting on me.

He daydreams but moves forward, almost in automatic mode. The crackling speaker whispers an old rock song. It's heavy, his hands are sweaty on the steering wheel.

The open window lets in a draft of hot air which whistles in his ears. Suddenly, small impacts on the cabin of his jalopy bring freshness...

- It's raining ! Finally ! he said to himself out loud

The windshield wipers squeal as his blood pressure drops again. The air becomes less suffocating.

(summer rain)

The impatient and distracted

They met on the networks. They got more, quickly, feelings in broadband. A first meeting is agreed. She, in advance, stomps with impatience. He, distracted, dragged on getting ready. She's been fooled too much and won't wait any longer. She blocks him on the app and goes home, annoyed. On his two-wheeled mount, he sees her leaving. He accelerates but does not see a car. Result: a broken leg and a failed love story.

While going through my closet, I found an old jacket. A bit spongey, mostly aged, with nice colors, a little tarnished. It still suits me, it's true that I haven't grown too much since I was sixteen. But it doesn't close anymore. I search pockets, by instinct, or intuition. I take out something soft and a little warm, lukewarm to be more precise. I recognize what it is. I used to wear it often... I adjust it to my face. It fits me, like the jacket... I'm going for a walk... with this memory of my childhood.

(find)

Head in the air as I am, I got caught up in my
thoughts...
Fall forward and here I am with my nose in
reality!
I wasn't ready!

*I seek my balance by relieving myself of excess salt
water.*
It's not the sea to drink...

Just a few tears...

A perpetual morose character, he walks the cobbled streets in silence. At the bend of an alley, a woman hanging on her phone starts laughing, in a tickling tone. These bursts of happiness caress his eardrums and crack the coldness of his face. His pouting lips form a smile, then, unable to contain it, he lets out a burst of laughter that stirs his ribs and soothes his heart. He continues his journey, changed.

She leaves her house, the rain has just stopped. The wet ground sings under her soles. It's harmless, she goes for bread. It's harmless, it's his morning routine. In front of the bakery, she searches her mind to find a smile to put on. In his head, it's still raining, always in fact. She comes in and says, "Hello."

I am a very consistent person...
It's just that I have a lot of variables!

Life is beautiful
Deep down, she looks like you
She has the echo of your smile
Its sky has the blue of your eyes
And I want to spend it with you

Worn out from being thrown from illusion to
disillusionment.
His eyes wash with a soap made of emotion.
What we call: sadness

*We will never get tired of hugging each other even
through the years we get tired of seeing each other
happy.*

They are no longer far. I move as quickly as possible. I slip on moss on the ground, lose my balance because of a root, my head telescopes a tree trunk. My right ear, at the forefront of the shock, burns and resonates. Barking! They released the dogs. Fear paralyzes my thoughts. I continue my run, panicked.

"Bam!" »

A gunshot rang out, quickly accompanied by others. I'm almost home... I slip into my burrow. My heart is pounding in my chest. The hunt is therefore already on.

In any case, it's too late, nothing will ever be the same again... He's trapped. Fingers clenched on the trigger... He takes a deep breath and presses... The bullet goes... hits... and leaves its target on the floor. There, on the ground lies his celibacy, while he sends a new message, his heart galloping, to accept the second date.

The stars are so many lighthouses that show us the dreamlike beaches of the field of possibilities of our dreams.

I think I'm a soft heart
Who has tough skin

The fine summer rain falls on his face. In the distance, in the path that has become muddy, the old bus finally appears. Her blood flow accelerates, she blushes, her thoughts race and sparkle. With narrowed eyes, she watches for the return of her beloved.

I don't know about you. But when my children were born and my eyes saw them for the first time. I already knew all their features, as if my heart had already contemplated them.

Prisoner of a whirlwind of light, she seeks a piece of darkness in which to hide. Cloistered in a bottomless darkness, he searches for a light to guide him. Shouldn't they meet?

He jumps with both feet into the smiling puddles of his happiness in order to splash the built wall of his regrets.

The stars were not aligned...
Their hearts undeniably were. Like comets, they collided.

The hunter and the bird

The hunter of the frosty lands, still his evil saber in hand, stamped with his heel the carcass of the majestic bird lying in the dust. He gave himself a grin to celebrate his victory. He already imagined himself spending the gold coins that the head of this beast would earn him. He raised his weapon to carry out his misdeed. But suddenly, the bird's eyes opened, releasing flames that ran through its entire body. With a quick blow of his beak, he decapitated his attacker.

As long as a small flame inhabits its heart, the phoenix is immortal.

To you who have given so much, the gardeners of the seeds of our existence.

We grow to flourish.

To brothers and sisters, by ties or by blood.

To all the rare beings, dear to our little patched-up thrills.

You left too soon...

infinitely too soon.

*The nightmares are
dreams
in a bad mood.*

You & me

We are the main ingredients of our happiness.

If I were a star?
First of all, I hope I don't get dizzy.
Then I would like to be the one who guides
insomniac sailors to safety...
or else...
better: the one who surprises the first kiss of clumsy
lovers!
Ah! If I were a star!

What if...
A day.
She was leaving, taking all her smiles with her.
I would become liquid...
And I would disappear...
Evaporating...

– Are you crying? For what ?
– It's the onions...
– But you don't cut it!
– No, but I think of my mother when she was
cutting it...

There are people who make a rocket with a
rubber band and two paper clips.
My grandmother made me happiness with two
eggs, flour and a little milk.
My heart still remembers

Did I really exist before you?
My most distant memory being that of being
snuggled in your arms.

The darkness is not thick enough to cover my
doubts...
 I stand there, weary... Denied by sleep...

A gentle and poetic breeze filled his mood. He longed to find his beloved. This desire was already a few pages old. Young romance hero lost between two chapters. Worried and uncertain of the author's intentions. He dove into his heart and found the courage to cross the blank page to the next chapter, whose peak he could make out in the distance.

Thus, perched on the title of it, he was able to observe himself embracing his other half in a beautiful reunion.

But he was still lost, our young hero, fatally unable to go back through the turned pages. What choice was available to him? Suicide or crime of passion? What was the difference?

A simple question of point of view.

Digging through the page, he retrieved the necessary ingredients and made up the word: poison. The dancing letters turned into a small vial. With trembling and feverish hands, he opened it and drank the contents. The effect was quick, he took one last look at his beloved entwined with his double... who was also dying.

Without understanding what was happening, this unfortunate, dejected heroine found herself alone. She shed all the tears in her heart. Then, as if filled with certainty, she got up and began the journey to the next chapter...

I don't shed tears
I pour out emotions

I am a colorblind painter with Parkinson's,
I don't respect the right colors and my features are
messy.
But I express what I feel and always deliver my
emotions

In all these aborted moments...
The parallel possibilities that would have changed
our beings.
The directions of life:
destiny or pure chance?

You & me

Love is a feeling
Joy, an emotion
We are the apotheosis of this emulsion

I have my feet on the ground to feel the world
turning...
My thoughts sail between the stars!

To write...
It's like reading...
But with the possibility of modifying the past,
present and future.

I don't like it when you're not there
The emptiness of your absence resonates within me.
Then this noise fades under the silence of our
reunion kiss

And then, one day I ran into her.
As we discover the moon when we look up on a
beautiful starry night.
And I started a dream...
Which became my reality.

A kiss doesn't weigh much, but it can tip the scales
of love.
Even reason is no match.

Embrace your destiny

On one knee on the ground, I listen attentively to the royal soothsayer. I feel the heavy gaze of the king weighing on my curved spine. He reluctantly took me out of jail. Irony of fate that our destinies. Me, locked up for an offered kiss, him, great king and helpless father. The enemy captured his daughter two moons ago. He lost a thousand men trying to recover it. The soothsayer, through a dream adorned with strange plants, saw that I was the princess's savior. It lists upcoming events. I learn that I will lose fingers, torn to pieces by wild beasts. He informed me that I would have one eye gouged out by a blow from a sword. He tells me that I will kill the kidnapper of the princess. I listen to the passage where I save her from the inferno that the enemy lair becomes. I accept the death he describes to me, prisoner in the flamcs, watching the princess saved but hysterical at losing me. The soothsayer is silent. The king orders me to leave. He entrusted me with two hundred men. I put on my helmet and leave the throne room. Ready to embrace my destiny, I set out to save my love.

The sweet ecstatic dream ends with a rustle as the conquered reader turns the last page. He sighs at having finished his book, without suspecting that it will live in him forever.

<u>Other works by the author:</u>
L'énigme de Charles Dufresne (roman)
L'école sous le phare (enfants)
Une goutte d'eau un peu salée (recueil)
Une petite bulle de pensées (recueil)
Pat Ethique l'anomalie colérique (recueil)

They are all available on Amazon but only in French

<u>To contact me:</u>
gerald.odar.auteur@gmail.com
Instagram @thelunaticanomaly.poetry
Facebook The lunatic anomaly poetry

It's your turn:

Cover photo by Hao Wang (Unsplash.com)

Printed by Amazon KDP

Made in the USA
Monee, IL
08 July 2026